Bill Huebsch

A Pastor's Guide to *Whole Community Catechesis*

TWENTY-THIRD PUBLICATIONS
185 WILLOW STREET • PO BOX 180 • MYSTIC, CT 06355
TEL: 1-800-321-0411 • FAX: 1-800-572-0788
E-MAIL: ttpubs@aol.com • www.twentythirdpublications.com

A Pastor's Guide to Whole Community Catechesis

Twenty-Third Publications
A Division of Bayard
185 Willow Street
P.O. Box 180
Mystic, CT 06355
(860) 536-2611 or (800) 321-0411
www.twentythirdpublications.com
ISBN:1-58595-376-8

Library of Congress Catalog Card Number: 2004109201
Printed in the U.S.A.

Contents

Introduction

A Pastor Writes...

I've been a priest for fourteen years. I've seen a lot of change in my ministry in these years. For the most part, the change has been good. More lay people than ever have come forth to serve the community. Many, many parishioners are committed to the parish. My own preaching has gotten better as I have matured. And even though there are fewer priests, we work more closely together than we did in the past.

I know my pastoral staff shares my sense that the Church is in good hands. The staff is more professional than ever; some share the same basic theological training that was once reserved only for candidates to the priesthood. The staff understands and appreciates the need for collaboration, for shared vision, and for open communication among us. They "get it" that the Church is only strong when we are united with our bishops and holy father. And they are ready and willing to take the risk of shifting gears and to change when necessary.

But what I want to tell you today is that nothing has been more exciting in my priesthood than the recent growth and reform of catechesis. A few years ago, only a few of the most active parishioners participated in adult faith formation. Today I have thousands who have experienced renewal. A few years ago, there was a serious departmentalization between liturgical and catechetical ministries. Today, they work together as one.

A few years ago, I honestly doubted how serious was the conversion to Christ of my parishioners. Today I hear them witness to and share their faith every single week. A few years ago it was like pulling teeth to fill needed parish volunteer ministries. Today people come forth because of their faith, willing to work. A few years ago, parishioners were contributing money at a slow pace, making support for the work of the Church difficult. Today the collections are up. When people know Christ, they become generous. A few years ago, if asked, I would have said that most of my parishioners were living in homes where very little faith was visible. Today, we're developing households of faith across the parish and the results are fantastic!

Building on recent papal documents (*Evangelii Nuntiandi* and *Catechesi Tradendae*, to be precise), those who are now helping us imagine and implement the possibilities that arise from the *General Directory for Catechesis* have brought new hope to me as a pastor, and new life to the parish where I serve.

I know it is a risk to change. But done carefully and well, this shift to catechesis for the whole community is worth it. I'm excited about this book, and I encourage you to read it from cover to cover. I hope it will help you see the tremendous possibilities for your parish once whole community catechesis is in place.

Thank you for the work you are doing today in your own parishes. We priests are fewer in number, a bit grayer at the hairline, and seasoned with the pain of the sexual misconduct cases. Despite this, I believe the Spirit is with us, stirring hearts in this catechetical renewal, and rising like a phoenix in today's Church.

Father Jan Kevin Schmidt is a priest of the Archdiocese of Cincinnati, and is pastor at Immaculate Heart of Mary Parish. He is the chaplain and a former religion faculty member of Archbishop McNicholas High School.

★1.

What Pastors Want

In this chapter you will read about the needs of pastors like yourself and see how whole community catechesis can answer these needs.

No Surprises!

When you ask them, pastors will tell you what they want for themselves and the parish communities they serve. They have a clear sense of what will work for them in their particular parishes, and what will not. And the pastoral associates who work with them know, too. Whether lay or ordained, they generally share the desires of the pastor.

And what pastors want will not surprise you. It doesn't take a rocket scientist to figure out the needs of a parish community. The late Bishop Ray Lucker of the New Ulm Diocese in Minnesota always said that "the ministry of the Church today is the same as the ministry of Christ." We start with that, and add to it the needed modern approaches that serve us best. Also, it will not surprise you that what pastors want is very reasonable.

★ They want the same things that their lay and ordained pastoral associates want.

★ Only a few have extreme right or left wing ideas.

★ Pastors are very faith-filled and hard working.

3

≋ **THE PASTOR WANTS...**
A Faith-Filled Parish

One pastor told me that all he really wants is for the folks in his parish to know Jesus and to love the Church. He hopes that all his efforts will lead to this. He knows, he told me, that leading a community where conversion is happening, where people are turning their hearts to Christ, will lead to a more grace-filled parish, and that would be positive and affirming for him and his staff.

Light a Fire!

> **Conversion precedes catechesis.**
>
> —*General Directory for Catechesis, #62*

One way to speak of this is to say that he wants to light a fire! The fire in the belly of the parish comes from deep faith in Christ. People who have encountered Christ, and who have continued to deepen their friendship and companionship with Christ, are active, generous, supportive, loving, forgiving, and feel their own call to ministry. And they have a *desire* for more. They want catechesis. They want to support their parish.

Pastors know this. But what they don't always know is how to help people experience this encounter with Christ. Parishes can play a significant role in helping people turn to Christ. And this turning is what makes parishioners "better Catholics." They come to their Catholic faith, to the sacraments and the parish, with real heart when they are rooted in Christ.

★ Conversion to Christ is the basis of strong Catholic faith.

★ Conversion of this kind leads to active parish members.

★ Parishes can help members experience this encounter with Christ.

◎ What Does WCC Offer?

Drawn as it is from the Christocentric approach enunciated in *Evangelii Nuntiandi* and *Catechesi Tradendae*, whole community catechesis (WCC) has conversion to Christ as the beginning point and as the ongoing goal. WCC initiates in the parish a lifelong process of turning to Christ, of falling in love with Christ, of putting on Christ like a garment over and over again.

≋ THE PASTOR WANTS…
Active Parishioners

All pastors want is for the members of their parishes to feel like this is their Church, too. It isn't "father's Church" anymore. They want folks to come forward to assist with the work of the parish, and to live in their homes as faithful people. They want them to be active in the community where the parish is located, to be publicly faithful when that is called for. In other words, they want an adult Church with a sense of ownership.

Sluggish Faith

But many members are content to remain uninvolved. They prefer to just let someone else do it all. Many parishes have the same fifteen or twenty, or maybe eighty or ninety, parishioners handling virtually all the parish work.

So What Choices Do You Have?

★ You could give up and become cynical and bitter.

★ You could keep hounding people until they give in.

★ Or you could get adults back into catechesis.

And it isn't only in parish programs that pastors want parish members to be active, it's also at the Sunday assembly for Mass. Often people just sit there, mumbling through the responses, watching what's happening, but participating only minimally. Or they attend only once in a while and really don't know the prayers of the Mass any more. Or sometimes it may feel as though they're simply and only fulfilling their obligation to be there, without much joy or deep faith.

⊚ What Does WCC Offer?

Whole community catechesis is no panacea. When people's faith is flat, it takes much work to re-energize it. But the Holy Spirit, working in people's hearts when we open the right doors for them, is more powerful than malaise. The Spirit trumps indifference, overcomes sluggish hearts and ignites a fire there. Whole community catechesis provides the right doors:

★ breaking open the word and faith sharing for everyone in the parish

★ parish-based retreats

★ adults learning with their children

★ a more powerfully participatory Sunday Mass

★ more well-developed households of faith.

≋ THE PASTOR WANTS...
Enough Money

Who doesn't want this? This is one of the most reasonable things a pastor wants. Parish budgets are generally low and staff salaries are probably lower (in most cases) than they should be. The pastor wants enough money, not so he looks good or is himself comfortable financially, but *so that the work of God can be done well.*

He wants enough to pay decent wages to parish ministers. He wants to provide programs to assist the poor. He wants to reach out to the ones whose faith has grown cold. He wants to keep the buildings in decent shape. And at the end of the month, he wants to save a little money for a rainy day.

◉ What Does WCC Offer?

Practitioners of whole community catechesis understand that poor stewardship is connected to undeveloped hearts. Where there is conversion, there is generosity with money. And whole community catechesis also turns on the idea, expressed in the *General Directory for Catechesis,* that conversion and catechesis work hand in glove. One leads to the other. And both lead to a desire for deeper life in the Church.

We're not saying here that whole community catechesis is some new form of fundraising. But in parishes where there is renewal of heart, where adults are being offered opportunities which give rise to the possibility of their ongoing conversion to Christ, the need for fundraising is greatly reduced.

≋ THE PASTOR WANTS...
A Well-Trained Staff

The amount of pastoral work at the parish level has increased in recent years. Where once it might have been possible mainly to prepare for the Sunday liturgy, manage the school and religious ed program, and deal with financial concerns, parishes today are providing a much wider range of services.

Parish members have come to expect excellence on the part of the parish staff. The pastor has become, in many cases, an executive in charge of many departments. Often these departments are in competition with each other for shares of the budget, for "air time" on Sunday during announcements, and for scarce volunteers. Sometimes this competition results in a level of departmentalization within the parish. The results? One hand doesn't know what the other hand is up to.

> **You are not alone!**
>
> Even though it might seem like it sometimes, you are not alone as pastor.
>
> The whole church is pulling for you. And whole community catechesis offers you a major helping hand!

Cooperation and Good Will

What the pastor wants is for all these parish workers and parish programs to work effectively together. He wants the parish to follow a single, well-developed mission. He wants less competition and more cooperation. And he wants the members of the parish, who only glimpse this activity from a distance, to be able to see the unity and cohesion in parish programs.

◉ What Does WCC Offer?

The beauty of whole community catechesis is that it provides the forum in which all parish ministries come together. Just as the Sunday assembly gathers all, regardless of their specific parish roles, so it is with whole community catechesis. It gathers all into catechesis assemblies in which all players in the parish have a role.

Those with the gift of teaching, teach. Liturgical and musical ministers lead prayer and music. Bakers and cooks, bake and cook and share the goodies with all. Those in pastoral care witness to the stories that unfold for them. The ones working for justice and peace witness to their service. Many people are table leaders, or welcomers, or play other roles. The pastor is present, as pastor. Young adults and youth members take active roles. Stewardship results from the conversion. Everyone grows. Everyone benefits. No one loses. Every adult is invited to learn. All the various separate ministries come together here, just as in the catechumenate, to say, in essence, "This is the parish. We are this local Church. Amen."

It's a unifying process, gathering the parish into one.

≋ THE PASTOR WANTS...
Less Conflict and More Harmony

Today we live in a polarized society, especially in the political arena where the right and left wings of the government seem further apart than ever. And in fact, they seem to like it that way, believing somehow that making themselves enemies of each other will get them elected.

Sometimes in the Church we get that way too. But what the pastor wants is for the Church to be less polarized and more in harmony with the central mission: doing Christ's work on earth. He wants unity. He wants folks to understand their faith because he knows that often, disagreement arises from ignorance of the real theology, the real practices of the Church.

◉ What Does WCC Offer?

More than anything else, catechesis is needed on many of the questions that divide the Church today. Why? Because when you examine the issues, we really aren't that far apart on most of these matters. The Catholic Church is big. It has room for everyone. It embraces dialogue, conversation, and the search for answers.

What if we offered catechesis on the Eucharist, bringing together those who want more perpetual adoration with those who think we should only pray the liturgy? And what if, in that catechesis, we found room for both sides? The Church is not a democracy. We don't decide which teachings we like and which we don't by catechizing about them. But in catechesis, deeper understanding leads to deeper mutual understanding.

When adults enter into ongoing catechesis, they come to understand the role of the teaching Church and of conscience, the role of Scripture and of Church tradition, the importance of adhering to Church teachings and the importance of prophetic examination of those teachings in light of today's world.

≋ THE PASTOR WANTS...
People Who Understand Their Faith

OK. So this probably seems self-evident by now. Pastors want parish members of all ages who understand their faith more deeply. They know that when people understand their faith, there is less division and more unity. There is more excitement for parish life. There is more chance that the ministries favored by Jesus will become a reality for your parish.

> **To be the pastor of an adult parish is the greatest joy in the world.**

To be the pastor of an adult parish is the greatest joy in the world. And doesn't that stand to reason? Who wants to pastor a flock that is hesitant, absent, in the background of parish life, reluctant to get involved, ignorant on many matters of faith, and slow to respond to his initiatives?

◉ What Does WCC Offer?

This is a place where WCC offers you a real tool. We've been trying to do good adult education in the Church for the last forty years. We haven't succeeded. By and large, this is because adults have told us they do not want to go back to classrooms for that learning.

Whole community catechesis succeeds because it gathers adults in an alternate setting, a more natural and personally safer setting. It gathers them in the same way we gather for Mass, into "catechesis assemblies." By gathering adults into these catechesis assemblies, which address their real interests and needs, and by launching efforts toward greater conversion in the parish, which lights a fire in people's hearts with love for Christ, and by making the Sunday assembly more and more participatory, whole community catechesis slowly creates adult parishes where people are growing to more mature faith.

Broaden the Goal

Whole community catechesis is not, strictly speaking, a shift to adult education. It is a shift from child-centered parish formation programs to ones in which the center broadens. Using your present children's program as a springboard, it opens real doors for adults to enter back into catechesis.

(To read more about this process, see chapter five in my book, *Handbook for Success in Whole Community Catechesis.* There you will find the exciting plans for exchanging the present "classroom" approach, which leaves most adults out in the cold, for the "assembly" approach, which has room at the table for everyone.)

〰 THE PASTOR WANTS...
Parishioners Who Are Excited About the Parish

Pastors want a parish with fire in its belly! On the face of it, such parishes may seem to some pastors like they'd be more work. Whole community catechesis helps people enter into a lifelong journey of faith. It deepens their commitment. This may lead to a discovery of more pressing spiritual needs. It may lead to households that try to find their way back to full, active membership. Folks who've met Christ may look for ways to serve within the Church. It may lead to a situation where many who are now mainly absent on Sunday morning, start showing up!

What a problem to have! And in fact, pastors *do want this*, deep down, even if it does mean more work. Because they know that they would also have a great number of ministers to help meet all those needs and wants. They'd have a supportive parish, on fire with love for Christ.

Whole community catechesis helps people enter into a lifelong journey of faith. It deepens their commitment.

◉ What Does WCC Offer?

But how do you light such a fire? Or better yet, what is this fire we're talking about in the first place? The fire is deep faith. It's people, many people within the parish, falling in love with Christ, walking with Christ in their daily lives, learning more and more what this means, and inviting others within their daily circle to do likewise. It's the outcome of evangelization.

These people are coming to see that the Church is their home. This is where they find support for their faith, in the sacraments, catechesis assemblies, prayer opportunities, and breaking open the word. This is where they learn to work for justice and peace, perform ministries of pastoral care, outreach, compassion, and love, and this is where they learn to reach out to the newcomer, the rejected, and the lonely.

By experiencing deep life within the Church they experience Christ. For Christ is the head of the body, the Church. One really can't come to know Christ without also coming to know the Body of Christ.

Ways to Light the Fire through WCC

★ Make "faith sharing" a part of every parish meeting

★ Make "households of faith" the goal of parish programs

★ Plan parish-based youth and adult retreats similar to Teens Encounter Christ (TEC), Search, or Cursillo

★ Give witness as pastor to your own faith

★ Schedule parish renewal programs that are carefully tailored to the needs of modern households

★ Offer programs that address the needs and situations of today's young adults

★ Plan assemblies that are exciting, enjoyable, and effective.

≋ THE PASTOR WANTS...
A Parish Where All Feel Welcome

People often come to see pastors or pastoral staff members when there is trouble in their lives. Most of the time, the pastor and staff are able to comfort and guide these folks without any conflict. But sometimes the Church's response may tend to be more legal than pastoral.

Pastors want to be able to offer people a pastoral solution rather than a merely legal one when they come with their lives falling apart. This is a big one for pastors. They don't want their hands tied. When people come to them, their lives in shreds for whatever reason, they don't want to offer them a stone. They want to offer them bread.

Really the "Pastor"

Pastors want more than anything to really "pastor." When folks are struggling, they want to guide them gently back to Christ and the Church. And they know that some people who are away from the Church are not away from Christ. In Christ's name, they want to welcome these people home.

⊚ What Does WCC Offer?

Making one's way into the heart of the parish community is slow work for many people. The catechesis assemblies offer a safe place for people to do that. By gathering with others on the journey of faith, in an environment where no one sticks out, where everyone fits in, a sense of security unfolds for people. They begin to see that the Church loves them, just as Christ did. They meet others in the parish in this setting. They meet pastoral staff people. And even if they don't feel they can worship at Sunday Mass, in a certain way, they are beginning to assemble with us. They're beginning to break down whatever barrier they experience.

Who are the people who feel unwelcome?

★ the divorced, who often feel outside the fold

★ those who remarried without an annulment who actually are outside the Church

★ people in ecumenical homes who often feel their partner isn't welcome

★ gay or lesbian folks who are under constant fear of being rejected

★ people from homes where there is abuse, violence, and addiction

★ former prisoners who often feel too much shame to return

★ people whose faith has grown cold and don't know where to turn

★ those who simply don't know much about the Church

★ many adults on the fringe have never received confirmation

★ people in the aftermath of abortion who believe the Church rejects them

★ people who are experiencing doubts about their faith

★ those who are angry with the Church for being too slow to reform (or too fast to reform).

≋ THE PASTOR WANTS...
To Be Thanked and Affirmed

In most parishes at the present time, pastors and most pastoral staff people have little or no role in religious education or catechesis. Meeting in classrooms of various kinds makes it very difficult for parish staff to be visible. The classroom model allows for only one or two people to serve as catechist.

But in whole community catechesis assemblies, the whole parish is catechist. "It takes a whole parish," someone recently told me, "to really catechize my child." The same is true for all of us. Having the assembly model in place provides avenues in which the pastor and pastoral staff of the parish can be seen, known, appreciated, and yes, thanked in public for their service.

Gratitude

We all know that pastors don't accept their vocations in order to have the accolades of the masses. Pastoral staff don't either. If that were the motive, the payoff would be a long time in coming. But nonetheless, providing a forum for gathering in which the parish leaders are received with gratitude builds up the whole community. It affirms everyone when the leaders are affirmed.

◎ What Does WCC Offer?

We're starting to repeat ourselves now. Whole community catechesis provides a method in which faith sharing, parish retreats, conversion to Christ, a connection to the Sunday assembly, and gatherings are used to welcome and comfort and educate the whole parish. This creates an environment where people come to appreciate and understand the pastor and staff in ways that our present model just doesn't provide.

≋ THE PASTOR WANTS...
To Be in Good Standing with His Bishop

The bishops are the "first teachers" of the Church and they want the people of their dioceses to know their faith, period. The bishops of the United States have made this clear by providing a process through which religion textbooks are found to be in conformity with the *Catechism of the Catholic Church*. But the bishops of today also recognize the wider need. If, for example, a child in the fourth grade, learns his or her lessons perfectly and can even recite them back verbatim, but...

★ has not had an encounter with Christ, or

★ goes home to a house where the faith is not cherished, or

★ is not a regular part of the Sunday assembly for Mass, or

★ is not encouraged to live his or her faith on a daily basis at home, or

★ the home is devoid of religious symbolism and language, or

★ the child does not witness the faith of his or her own parents or guardians,

...the bishops know that the *seed is falling on rocky ground*. It will not take root and grow. Growth in faith will not be lifelong.

What Bishops Want

So to really be in good standing with the bishops, pastors know deep down they must cultivate a lively faith community, rich with households living a daily faith, devoted to the Sunday assembly for Mass, deeply committed to Catholic social teachings. Pastors know this. It isn't enough merely to have an adequate way to teach "about religion." Much more is needed in order to achieve what the bishops want.

◉ What Does WCC Offer?

Whole community catechesis offers the "more" that is needed. Test scores and understanding about religion actually rise when the context feels "more like Mass than class." So merely having a Catholic school or an organized religious ed program, will not do the trick. We need a studied effort to help people meet Christ and understand their faith better.

★2.

On Whose Authority?

In a nutshell, here is how the ideas about whole community catechesis came into the mainstream of Catholic life throughout the world in the past several years.

Papal and International Documents

At the Second Vatican Council, there was not much debate about catechesis, but it was generally agreed at that time that we did not do very adequate catechesis within the Church. In fact, we primarily worked with children, asking them to memorize verbatim answers to questions from the Church's catechism.

In fact, at the Council, the only meaningful reference to catechesis came in article forty-four of the "Decree on the Pastoral Office of Bishops in the Church." There it called for a series of "general directories" to be drawn up after the Council. These were to address, for example, the care of souls, the pastoral care of special groups, "and also a directory for the catechetical instruction of the Christian people in which the fundamental principles of this instruction and its organization will be dealt with...."

Renewal Was Underway

The Council Fathers were aware that a catechetical renewal was underway. The search had begun "for a better method than the questions and answers of the catechism," as Sr. Kate Dooley pointed out in an essay published in *The Echo Within* (Notre Dame: Ave Maria Press, 1997). In the early 1900s, catechetical leaders meeting in southern Germany were testing new methods. They recognized that merely knowing facts about the faith was not the same as encountering Christ and hearing the Gospel proclaimed!

Recapturing the Vision

The so-called "kerygmatic movement" of the 1950s went even further, moving us "to recapture the spirit and vision of the Church of the apostolic and patristic era" (Dooley). This movement added the element of "formation" to the memorized catechism. Learners received the proclamation of the Gospel, the teachings of Jesus and the saving acts of his life, death, and resurrection.

This movement was based on four "signs" that were to be in balance if a proper understanding of the faith was to be the result:

★ liturgy

★ Scripture

★ Church teaching

★ the witness of Christian living.

A Deeper Faith

"Catechesis was no longer limited to instruction and to the classroom" (Dooley). Instead, it merged with liturgy, biblical study, and discipleship into an organic whole, just as it was experienced in the early Church. We are grateful to Josef Jungmann, SJ (1889–1975), who taught pastoral theology on the faculty of the University of Innsbruck, for these insights which are part and parcel of all effective catechesis today.

In the United States, Jungmann's work was popularized by Johannes Hofinger (1905–1984). It was mainly through Hofinger's efforts that a series of international catechetical study weeks were held in

★ Nijmegen, 1959

★ Eichstatt, 1960

★ Bangkok, 1962

★ Katigondo, 1964

★ Manila, 1967

★ Medellin, 1968.

These study weeks, as you can see, anticipated Vatican II and continued during and after it. They had influence on the Council itself. The Eichstatt week had particular influence as it laid out principles of liturgical and catechetical renewal. But it was at Medellin, Columbia, in 1968, that serious reflection on evangelization led to a new focus. It was seen during the week in Medellin that we cannot presuppose faith in members of the Church. Baptism is no guarantee that people have come to encounter Christ and adhere to him and the Church with their whole hearts.

After Vatican II

In 1971, Pope Paul VI published the *General Catechetical Directory*, which provided a framework on which a great deal of catechetical renewal was built. This directory reflected all the work done to that point at the various study weeks and at the Council. This first general directory was enculturated in the United States by way of a pastoral message issued by the U.S. Catholic bishops in 1972, called "To Teach as Jesus Did," which provided impetus for much growth in catechesis in this country.

In 1974, an international synod of bishops dealt in great depth with the question of evangelization, but they did not publish any outcomes. Instead, they encouraged Pope Paul VI to reflect on their findings which he did, publishing an apostolic exhortation in 1975, *Evangelii Nuntiandi* or, in English, "On Evangelization in the Modern World." This document was received with tremendous grace by the Church. At the time, it was certainly the most important document issued in the Church since the close of Vatican II. It is concise (only five chapters long), vibrant, readable, and profound. In article four Paul VI posed important questions. They voice thoroughly modern concerns, rooted in today's situation. They are challenging, Christocentric, and focused on the Gospel, the *kerygma*. He asked: *Do we have conviction? Is there freedom of spirit? And, mainly, are we effective?*

At this turning point of history, does the Church or does she not find herself better equipped to proclaim the Gospel and to put it into people's hearts with conviction, freedom of spirit, and effectiveness?

—Pope Paul VI, Evangelii Nuntiandi, article 4

Whole community catechesis arises from the GDC. The name itself, "whole community" comes from article 254 where it says:

The whole Christian community is the origin, locus, and goal of catechesis. Proclamation of the Gospel always begins with the Christian community and invites [people] to conversion and the following of Christ.

John Paul II

In 1977, a second international synod of bishops met in Rome with catechesis as its focus, no doubt preparing to draw up that directory which had been called for in article forty-four of the document on bishops at the Council. As the synod ended, the bishops issued a message to the people of God regarding their findings, and they also sent a set of resolutions to Pope Paul VI. Two years later, in 1979, Pope John Paul II issued the apostolic exhortation, *Catechesi Tradendae*, or in English, "On Catechesis in Our Time."

This exhortation laid the groundwork for a high-level renewal of catechesis in today's Church. It begins by reiterating what Paul VI had said earlier, that catechesis is Christocentric and it is rooted in tradition. Evangelization is the overarching activity, and catechesis is one dimension of that. The main sources, as directed by Vatican II's *Dei Verbum* ("The Dogmatic Constitution on Divine Revelation"), are Scripture and tradition. It also treats various practical aspects of catechesis and concludes by saying, in essence, that catechesis isn't just for children; *it's for everyone.*

More Key Statements

Two other key documents laid more groundwork.

★ the *Rite of Christian Initiation of Adults* in 1988

★ the *Catechism of the Catholic Church* in 1992.

Then in 1997, with the approval of Pope John Paul II, the *General Directory for Catechesis* was published. Drawing on the wisdom and spirit of all the work mentioned above, and much that is not mentioned here for the sake of brevity, the GDC provides sound, workable principles on which we can base our current work in catechesis.

The Church in the United States

The U.S. Catholic bishops have taken up both the spirit and the letter of the international and papal documents with great fervor. Writing in 1999 in *Our Hearts Were Burning Within Us*, the bishops said this

> We, as the Catholic bishops of the United States, call the Church in our country to a renewed commitment to adult faith formation, positioning it at the heart of our catechetical vision and practice. We pledge to support adult faith formation without weakening our commitment to our other essential educational ministries. This pastoral plan guides the implementation of this pledge and commitment (#6).

They Mean Business

The bishops are serious. Here in the United States, we are seeking a way for parishes to bring adults into the circle of catechesis within each parish. We want to provide formation for the whole community. It is not a shift away from children. It is a shift to a wider circle, a more inclusive method which adults as well as children will appreciate.

By the way, there are many excellent resources to help you make this shift to a whole community approach. Here are three:

★ Leader's Guide to *Our Hearts Were Burning Within Us* (United States Catholic Conference of Bishops)

★ *Nurturing Adult Faith: A manual for parish leaders* (National Conference for Catechetical Leadership)

★ *Handbook for Success in Whole Community Catechesis* (Twenty-Third Publications)

Solid Leadership

Also within the United States, there are many professional and dedicated men and women who head these diocesan offices:

★ religious education

★ catechesis

★ evangelization

★ faith formation

★ youth ministry

★ young adult ministry

★ family life and catechesis

★ the catechumenate

★ media

★ adult education

★ and whatever else they may be called.

These men and women have also been deeply involved with the renewal within the American Church. They are providing resources, study days, support, clearinghouses, coordination, and many other needed roles as this renewal unfolds at the parish level.

US Catholic Conference of Bishops

The staff and committees of the United States Catholic Conference of Bishops (USCCB) have also shown tremendous leadership in the years since this renewal has gotten underway.

★ Fr. John Hurley, CSP, of the Office for Evangelization, has led the way in keeping the Christocentric nature of catechesis ever before us. His own study days and institutes have provided an ever deeper appreciation of what evangelization means to the Church in the U.S. where Protestant evangelism is such a public force.

★ During her tenure there, Sr. Maureen Shaughnessy, SC, led the work in developing a focus on adult faith formation at the Office for Adult Catechesis.

★ The staff and members of the ad hoc committee which oversees the use of the Catechism in the US Church, headed by Msgr. Dan Kutys, have provided invaluable and time-consuming services to publishers of textbooks. We now have access to fine texts with which we can provide catechesis to the whole community, based on life-long learning models and sound theology.

★ Dan Mulhall has helped conduct a public conversation about this shift to catechesis for the whole community. He works in the Office for Catechesis.

★ Finally, Paul Henderson, who heads the publications arm of the USCCB, has upgraded the look and feel of many official publications, making them more accessible to more people.

★ The rest of the USCCB staff has also been strong and supportive as we come to understand together how to make this shift gracefully in the American context.

Catholic Higher Education

In Catholic colleges and universities as well, scholars have been working around the clock to help shape and reshape catechesis for our time. The leaders here are too numerous to mention all by name, but surely Dr. Jane Regan of Boston College whose seminal work on whole community catechesis, both in actual parish practice and theory, was crucial. Her colleague, Dr. Tom Groome, has been a leader in his own right. He recently wrote that for today's Church, where we understand faith to be a response of the whole person, "nothing less than *total catechetical education* will suffice" (emphasis his).

Early Leaders

Both Regan and Groome, however, also have others to thank as well. All of us were formed by the work of Francoise Darcy-Berube, John Westerhoff, and Maria Harris, who called for this catechetical shift. I've already mentioned Sr. Kate Dooley from Catholic University. But her colleagues there, Fr. Berard Marthaler, OFM, and Fr. Peter Phan have also been leaders.

Major conferences have begun to focus on this as well. Tim Ragan who organizes the East Coast Conference for Religious Education each winter in Washington, DC, devoted the entire 2004 conference to this renewal. The LA Religious Education Congress devoted dozens of workshops to it. Regional conferences around the nation are focused on it. Various organizations such as the National Conference for Catechetical Leadership (NCCL), National Catholic Education Association (NCEA), and the National Parish Catechetical Directors (NPCD), as well as evangelization conferences, liturgical gatherings, and even stewardship conferences see the need for parish-wide renewal in whole community catechesis as the basis of an adult Church.

Two Generations of Leadership

The list goes on and on. For two generations we have been talking about the need to make this shift, based on papal documents, international catechetical study weeks, the leadership of our own bishops, academics, diocesan and parish leaders, and publishers. Here is a sample of what some have had to say:

A lifelong journey

"For so long the Church
   thought of catechesis
   as something only for children.
We were forgetting that
   God's desire for our growth
   into holiness of life is never-ending,
   that our hearts are restless
   until they rest in God (St. Augustine).
The journey of faith is lifelong,
   and is ever in need of being
   nurtured and educated.
The developmental psychologists
   have amplified this point
   by describing stages
   in faith development
   that stretch from birth into eternity."

—Francoise Darcy-Berube,
Religious Education at a Crossroads

The liturgical connection

"Catechesis is gradual and ongoing;
    it takes place in and through the Christian community
    in the context of the liturgical year
      and is solidly supported
      by celebrations of the word."
        —Kate Dooley, OP, "Evangelization and Catechesis:
    Partners in the New Millennium," from *The Echo Within*

The real challenge

"The real challenge contained
    in the pursuit of alternative models
    is to create a radical new paradigm of catechesis.
It cannot simply be a process of going back to the past
    or making surface modifications
    of the present models."
      —Richard Reichert, "Alternative Models of Catechesis:
    Some Reflections" NCCL *Update* No. 7, April 1994

Suppertime!

"'Won't you stay for supper?'
The Christian greeting that matters most."
         —Bill Huebsch,
    Whole Community Catechesis in Plain English

Discovering Christ

"Discovering Christ is the finest adventure of your life.
　　But it is not enough to discover him just once.
Discovering him means to seek him always,
　　to come to know him through prayer,
　　participating in the sacraments,
　　meditating on his Word,
　　through catechesis and listening
　　to the teachings of the Church.
This is our most important task,
　　as St. Paul had well understood when he wrote:
　　　'For me, indeed, to live is Christ.'" (Philippians 1:21).

—Pope John Paul II,
Speech at Compostela, Spain, August 1989

The catechist

"Why do catechists catechize?
It is not just to transfer knowledge and teachings.
It is to call others to be witnesses and disciples
　　of Jesus Christ.
Of course, this requires
　　that our catechists be witnesses and disciples…
If catechists have not experienced an encounter with Jesus,
　　how can they "talk the talk"
　　　with other people? …
If they have encountered the Lord personally,
　　they can't keep that a secret."

—Fr. John Hurley, CSP,
Director of the Office for Evangelization, USCCB

Creating a home

"Parents have the first responsibility
    for the education of their children.
They bear witness to this responsibility
    first by *creating a home* where tenderness,
        forgiveness,
        respect,
        fidelity,
        and disinterested service are the rule...."
           —*Catechism of the Catholic Church,*
           Article 2223 (italics theirs)

Households of faith

"Parents [or guardians] are, in fact,
    the first and foremost educators
    of their children
    within a household atmosphere
        animated with love
        providing a well-rounded formation.
The household can be called the first school
    of those social virtues
    which every society needs.
The Christian household is enriched
    by the grace of the sacraments
    and is the place where children are first taught
        to know and love God
        and to know and love their neighbor.
Here they come to understand human companionship,
    here they're introduced into civic life,
        and here initiated into the parish community."
  —"The Declaration on Christian Education" from Vatican II,
    Article 3 from *Vatican II in Plain English,* by Bill Huebsch

The domestic Church

"The household is defined by Vatican II
  as a *domestic church*....
The members of the household
  pass on human values
  in the Christian tradition,
  and awaken a sense of God in its youngest members.
They teach the first tentative steps of prayer,
  they form the moral conscience,
  and they teach human love
    as a reflection of divine love.
Indeed, the catechetics of the household
  are more witness than teaching,
  more occasional than systematic,
  and more daily than structured into periods."

—Article 255, from *The GDC in Plain English*,
by Bill Huebsch

The bottom line

"The parish is the catechist."

—Msgr. Richard Burton,
Pastor, St. Anthony Parish, Washington, DC

Turning hearts to Christ

"The baptismal catechumenate is first and foremost
   about bringing participants
   into relationship with Jesus Christ
   and helping them turn to him
   with their whole hearts.
Is this task the first priority of the catechetical programs
   in our parish or school?"

—Christopher Weber,
Catechetical Leadership, Volume 12, No. 2

Intergenerational catechesis

"Hope for renewing an intergenerational vision
   and nurturing intergenerational learning
   is not beyond our reach.
We, are, by nature, intergenerational…
Our "school-mode" applications of religious education
   lead to more cognitively focused "classrooms."
This approach can lead to a de-emphasis on the affective
   and behavioral dimensions of learning and produce
   children who can recite prayers and Church doctrine,
   but who have little or no commitment to Church…
Intergenerational learning is by its nature
   experiential and relational."

—Steven Ellair, from an NCEA Scholars paper

The need for reform

"The current programmatic and age-specific approach
    to childhood and adolescent faith formation
    that has characterized the efforts of so many parishes
        over the past thirty years,
        is simply not adequate.
It may be one of the models of faith formation in a parish,
    but it cannot be the only model.
It is time to broaden our vision and our practice."

—John Roberto, *Generations of Faith*

One parent's viewpoint

"I'll tell you what.
    I'm worried about the religious ed program at St. Joe's,
    mainly because my kids *dread* going every week.
They beg not to go,
    and I can't blame them.
They spend all day in school
    and then get sent to a cold parish classroom
    with a strange teacher
    who drags them through the entire lesson in the textbook
    as though the goal of catechesis
    is to get to the end of the damn chapter!
And I'll tell you what,
    this isn't the fault of (the director at that parish).
It's the fault of the system.
She's doing the best she can
    but they expect miracles from her."

—The parent of a fifth-grade student at a New York-area
        parish in a 1999 interview with Bill Huebsch

Active engagement

"Those to be catechized cannot be passive recipients
    but must be actively engaged in the process
        through prayer,
        participation in the sacraments,
        the liturgy,
        parish life,
        social commitments,
        works of charity,
        and the promotion of human values.
Catechesis, after all, is a process of taking on
    a way of life and personal conversion,
        not the acquisition of a body of information."
                                —Article 157, from *The GDC in Plain English,*
                                            by Bill Huebsch

Adult Christians of mature faith

"Catechesis has always been much more—
        oh so much more!—
        than the handing down of doctrine.
It has always been more than a body of
        categorized knowledge to be retained.
The ultimate goal of all catechesis, after all,
        is adult Christians of mature faith."
                                —Cullen Schippe, La Jolla Conference, 1999

The whole community

"You cannot talk about religious education
        except as a process involving the whole community...."
                                —Fr. Peter Phan, La Jolla Conference, 1998

Brain friendly learning

"Religious education...includes giving reasons and explaining.
    But it also includes teaching by communities
    in nonverbal ways
    and teaching by the nonhuman universe."
                              —Gabe Moran (with Maria Harris),
                                    Reshaping Religious Education

Real life evangelization

"I used to know a family that only attended Mass occasionally.
This was in the 1950s when everyone went to Mass every week,
    unless they had a really good excuse not to.
Over the years, all the pastors in that parish
    tried every trick in the book
    to get this family to be more active in the Church.
Nothing worked.
Then a pastor was assigned to this parish
    who tried something new.
The first thing he did was to invite them to dinner.
He cooked the meal himself,
    he met them at the door, they shared a glass or two of wine,
    and other guests were invited, too.
Then they sat down at the table together and dined
    and he never once mentioned
    their relationship to the parish.
The truth is, he didn't really care.
What he cared about was this meal
    and their comfort in his home.
They came to Mass the following weekend
    and have been active ever since. Enough said."
                        —The pastor of a suburban Minneapolis parish
                            in a 1999 interview with Bill Huebsch

The work of the whole church

"Catechesis always has been and always will be a work
    for which the whole Church
    must feel responsible and wish to be responsible."
            —Pope John Paul II, *Catechesi Tradendae*, 1979

The gift of teaching

"We have gifts that differ according to the grace given to us:
    prophecy, in proportion to faith;
    ministry, in ministering;
    the teacher, in teaching;
    the exhorter, in exhortation;
    the giver, in generosity;
    the leader, in diligence;
    the compassionate, in cheerfulness."
                —Paul's letter to the Romans 12:6–8

The vocation of the catechist

"Within [the] common vocation of all the faithful,
    some of us are called specifically to be catechists.
The recent catechetical documents
    affirm that the vocational call of the catechist
    'is a specific call from the Holy Spirit'
    (Guide for Catechists, #2)
    through which 'the Church awakens and discerns
    this divine vocation
    and confers the mission to catechize' (GDC, #231)."
        —Jeanne Schrempf, director, Office for Evangelization and
                        Catechesis, Diocese of Albany

Today's needs

"Just as an artist needs the right tools
to create a masterpiece,
we as partners in ministry
need the right tools for engaging
the whole community
in lifelong catechesis."
—Diane Lampitt, president, Harcourt Religion Publishers

Adults in the process

"Imagining an alternative vision of catechesis,
one in which the adult community
is invited into the process of transformation,
is the first step that needs to be taken
as we move into the next millennium."
—Jane Regan "Catechesis for the Next Millennium:
Focus on Adults," from *Listening*, Winter, 1998

We are community

"Foundational to all of this
   is an ecclesiology of communion.
We are called to a *communio* of ordered relationships....
This brings us to understanding the parish
   as a web of interlocking relationships
   all focused on the community
      as a learning, questioning, celebrating, welcoming
      and evangelizing community of faith.
Key to developing whole community catechesis
   is visionary and shared leadership
   that holds out promise, hope,
      and which inspires the new."
      —Edith Prendergast, RSC, director, Office of Religious
      Education, Archdiocese of Los Angeles

Waiting with hope

"In all my years as catechist,
   DRE, editor, and publisher,
   I have hoped for a way to involve parents
      in adult faith formation
      that would not separate them
      from their children.
Whole community catechesis
   brings families together;
      it gets them talking about what they believe;
      it fires them up for Christ.
Just there, on the horizon,
   my hope is being realized."
      —Gwen Costello, publisher, Twenty-Third Publications

We want you to grow

"Whole community catechesis
  creates a path
  toward living discipleship.
The journey for those who follow Christ
  is more fruitful
  when we travel together,
  learning and growing,
  sharing and supporting
  one another along the way.
As the community reflects
  on its relationship in Christ,
  every member is nurtured in faith,
  newcomers and long-timers alike.
Each person is valued
  in a manner that says
  'not only do we care for you,
  but we care for you so deeply
  that we want you to grow
  in your love for Christ
  for the rest of your life.'"

—Leisa Anslinger,
Here Comes Everybody!
Whole Community Catechesis in the Parish

A new priority

"For many adults today, the local parish
　　has become irrelevant to their growth in faith.
Yet the *General Catechetical Directory* reminds us that
　　the parish is 'the most important *locus*
　　　　in which the Christian community
　　　　is formed and expressed' (#257).
The *Directory* also recognizes
　　that if the parish is to be a true center
　　of life and faith,
　　realistic attention
　　to the faith needs of adults
　　will have to become a priority."

　　　　　　　　　　　　　—Jo McClure Rotunno,
　　　　　　　　　　　　　Heritage of Faith:
　　　　　A Framework for Whole Community Catechesis.

What You Can Do As Pastor

There's a funny simile that has always seemed appropriate to those of us who work in Church ministry. The late Bishop Ray Lucker used to mention it to me. He'd say, "We have to be careful to tend to our own souls or we'll be like the shoemaker's children who go barefoot. Shoes for everyone else, but none at home."

We want catechesis for everyone. We want everyone to share their faith. But do we ourselves do so? *Are we in catechesis?* If indeed catechesis is part of lifelong learning and is constitutive of the Christian life, then perhaps the way to bring other adults of the parish into this circle is to stand there first ourselves.

This is true for the whole parish and school staff, including pastors and other priests. And it even includes the local bishop.

> **We aren't "doing" catechesis for people; we're sharing it with them.**

If we leaders aren't in catechesis ourselves, how can we expect others to see a need for it?

You can really help establish whole community catechesis by showing up at events and taking your place at a table, just like everyone else is expected to do. Don't float around the edges of the room, watching but not participating. And don't let the rest of your staff do that either. We aren't "doing" catechesis for people. We're sharing it with them. We're part of it ourselves.

If you sit down, take part in the learning, do the exercises, and share like everyone else, everyone will see your example and follow it. But if you think this is for others but not for you, people will follow that, too.

Share Your Own Faith

Recently, I was visiting a parish where they were engaged in breaking open the Word on a parish-wide basis. (For more on how to do this, see *The Handbook for Success in Whole Community Catechesis.*) The pastor was sitting there in the meeting with everyone else. The Gospel reading was from one of Jesus' sermons in Luke. The Question of the Week for sharing was, "When you heard the list of Beatitudes in today's Gospel, which one of them really hit you?" Around the table, each shared in turn. When it came to the pastor, he said,

> Well, you all know that I'm unmarried and live alone. My brother, George, was my best friend. And you know that I'm coming up on the second anniversary of his death. Losing him was like having an arm cut off in an accident. You stop bleeding, you heal sort of, but you never get the arm back. Today when I heard those words, "Blessed are you who weep...." I thought, "That's me." But then I thought about the second line, "for you will laugh," and I remembered that there is hope.

Simple. It took thirty seconds. He didn't preach. He'd done his preaching on the previous Sunday. By becoming "one of the members of the community" for that moment, he did not diminish his priesthood but rather made himself a leader. He modeled for others what he himself believed all should do: share faith because in sharing we find ourselves converted once again to Christ.

All of Us

Cardinal Roger Mahony of Los Angeles himself led faith sharing like this during the 2004 Religious Education Congress in Anaheim. He saw firsthand that breaking open the Word together releases the power of the Gospel through the Holy Spirit into peoples' hearts—and that has its own power to renew us and the whole Church.

You can really help the conversion process in your parish by jumping in with both feet and sharing your own faith as Cardinal Mahony and the pastor above did. Both especially helped those at the table who find it hard to share, as well as those who want to believe their faith is private.

Hire Only Those Who Have Met Christ

This is a key element. Parish and school staff people who are committed to Christ in their own lives become very strong leaders in whole community catechesis. Why? Because, as the popes and bishops have been saying now for more than three decades, catechesis is so Christocentric. It's about knowing Christ and living that faith in the Church.

The *General Directory* says it plainly: "Jesus Christ not only transmits God's word; Jesus *is* that word and all catechesis is completely tied to him" (from article 98, emphasis mine).

So if you hire a highly qualified staff person for liturgy, education, pastoral care, or any other purpose, even if they're the best in their field, but they aren't deeply committed in their faith, you do not help the process of inviting the whole community to renewal.

You can really help whole community catechesis become firmly established by providing time and encouragement for your staff to make annual retreats: your own parish–based retreats, TEC, Cursillo, directed retreats, or really any retreat that renews their faith.

Be In Conformity with the Catechism

This might seem like a minor contribution from you as pastor, but it is really important. There is a temptation on some parish staffs to make up their own curriculum for catechesis. It seems cheaper than buying all those textbooks every year. And besides, some staff people might think, 'what do the publishers know about all this anyway that I don't know?'

In whole community catechesis, we strongly recommend, however, that parishes and schools use texts that have been found to be in conformity with the *Catechism*. Why? Left to ourselves, any one of us would develop curriculum that would be not quite complete in some way. It would reflect our own biases and interests and abilities to teach it.

For example, some might not include much about the Blessed Virgin Mary, devotions to her, the rosary, and feast days. Mary just occupies a slightly less central place in many people's piety today. But a child or adult studying the faith has a *right* to learn about Mary and how we revere her. Others might not include enough material on Catholic social teaching, on liturgical catechesis, or on any other dimension of our faith.

Our First Teachers

As our first teachers, the bishops have solved this for us by providing us with excellent resources and textbooks which, according to their judgment, in terms of the scope of the content and the sequence in which it is presented, are in conformity with the *Catechism*. These textbooks by themselves are not the whole curriculum. But they're a necessary part of what we do. You can really help catechesis in your parish remain comprehensive and systematic by asking your staff to use books that are in conformity.

Extend a Hearty, Generous "Welcome!"

Finally, there is one more thing you can do. We said before that many of the households registered in your parish are not active. But—and this is a big "but"—that inborn hunger for God is still there. Christ still loves them and calls them home. Within their own hearts, people *know*. Deep down, they know they want to be connected to the Church and their faith.

But many of them simply do not feel welcome or don't know how to make their way back. Their faith has gone cold, perhaps. Or they feel they have some impediment that makes returning impossible. Yet they want their kids to "get some religion." They do know how important all this is, even if they just can't get to it in their own lives. Maybe they anesthetize themselves with TV, food, activity, work, or drugs and just keep their faith on the back burner.

Christ Still Loves Them

You can really help them—and the whole community—understand how much Christ loves them by offering them a huge, generous welcome whenever you have the chance. First welcome them back to the Sunday assembly. Once they're back, once they're present more often, you can help them work out whatever impediments there might be to receiving communion.

One of the results of catechesis assemblies in the whole community catechesis process is that people come to the surface of the parish who have been submerged for a long time. Suddenly there they sit, safely with their kids at one of the tables in the assembly hall, participating in catechesis. They might not even be coming on weekends to Mass yet, but there they are. This is a golden moment, a sacred moment, when you can offer them bread rather than a stone.

St. Monica's Parish

St. Monica's Parish in Santa Monica, California, tried something this past Easter that really worked. As part of the entrance procession, they used a song and spoken words to help folks understand that, indeed, *all are welcome*. This really is Christ's table here. Nothing really can separate us from the love of God in Christ Jesus. Nothing. On the following pages you'll find the text they used. It's strong, clear, and convincing. It uses that great song by Marty Haugen, "All Are Welcome" (GIA Publications). And not only does it welcome folks, it also at the same time catechizes the whole assembly to understand that they are welcome.

The parish solved the question of who's welcome to receive the Eucharist by inviting everyone present to come forward in the communion procession, but to simply place a hand over their heart if they are not partaking. This is also very welcoming. It's hard to be in the assembly on Sunday and then just sit there when everyone else gets up to receive. This allows all present to come forward and join in the procession. And it allows people to sort out their own consciences, as we are all called to do before receiving communion, so that even people who might regularly receive, on a given Sunday, may choose not to.

Msgr. Lloyd Torgerson, the pastor at St. Monica's, is one of the leaders of this movement. Here is the processional hymn they used.

Litany of Saints

Lector Who are you?

Are you married with kids, worrying for them and committed to their welfare?

Are you divorced?

Are you married for the second, or even the third time?

Are you a single parent struggling to make ends meet?

Are you gay or lesbian?

Well if you are, then you belong to us because you belong to Christ.

Refrain All are welcome, all are welcome,

All are welcome in this place.

Lector Are you lonely?

Are you a widow or widower?

Are you a single man or woman who would prefer to have a spouse?

Are you disabled or disfigured?

Does your life seem flat?

Is your faith on a slowdown?

Well, if you are, then you belong to us because you belong to Christ!

Refrain All are welcome, all are welcome,

All are welcome in this place.

Lector   Are you struggling financially?

Have you been laid off?

Out of work because of downsizing?

Does it seem like you can never quite get it all together?

Well, if so, then you belong to us because you belong to Christ!

Refrain   All are welcome, all are welcome,

All are welcome in this place.

Lector   Are you struggling with questions about family planning?

Have you been a victim of abuse or violence, of a crime?

Are you a criminal who has been imprisoned?

Do you have a past about which you feel ashamed?

Are you homeless or hopeless?

Well, if so, then you belong to us because you belong to Christ!

Refrain   All are welcome, all are welcome,

All are welcome in this place.

Lector   Are you new here? An immigrant maybe?

Are you from another Christian tradition?

Are you full of doubt today?

Are you fearful like the disciples were?

Has it been a while since you darkened the doorway of this church?

None of that matters. You belong to us because you belong to Christ.

Pastor   The Good News is that Christ is the host here today and he welcomes you as part of his body. The words from the Gospel are addressed to you: Peace be with you.

Refrain   All are welcome, all are welcome,

All are welcome in this place.

Epilogue

In some ways, I'm sure being a pastor is a real joy in today's Church. But I'm sure in other ways that you bear a very real burden. The work is hard. The money is always too tight. People don't always appreciate what happens. You are pulled in two directions, one by those who want more change and the other by those who want to go back to the good old days before Vatican II.

You're already so busy that you don't even take your day off regularly. I'm sure some days you must wonder how you got into this in the first place. But do you know what? *We need you.* We need healthy, holy priests like you. All of us do. Whether parish staff, parents of children, those in spiritual or personal crisis, your bishop, or just ordinary parishioners like me, we need you. Thank you so much for all your work and faith. Thank you for giving your entire life for us, for this ministry. As a priest, I'm sure you are constantly thanking others for helping in the parish, but it is we who should be thanking you.

And above all, thank you for taking on the work of renewing catechesis and the whole parish. You pastors around the nation are among the real heroes of whole community catechesis. You're sticking your neck out, taking the risk of leadership, and showing the way to others.

I think of Father Bob Deland in the Diocese of Saginaw. He's a busy guy, with duties outside the parish and within the diocese, plenty of work, but he sees the vision and knows what this renewal will do.

Or Father Jarlath Dolan at Padre Serra Parish in the Archdiocese of Los Angeles. It's a big parish, with a huge staff and many demands, yet he knows that sharing faith and building the whole community is the only way.

Or Father Mike Tauke at St. Mary's in Waverly, Iowa, in the Archdiocese of Dubuque. He can plainly see that whole community catechesis is the way of the future Church and, with his pastoral staff, he is moving forward with vigor.

Or Father Pat Apuzzo from St. Gabriel's Parish in the Diocese of Richmond. He stood up at the East Coast Conference for Religious Education in 2004 and said, speaking to the other priests in the room: "Fathers, I'm here to tell you, it's worth the risk."

Or my own pastor, Father Michael Lyons here in the Diocese of Duluth. It's a small town, and the parish doesn't have much staff, but he has a deep desire to renew the parish in Christ.

The list goes on and on, and by mentioning just a few, I don't mean to leave any of you off this list.

So thank you again. Thanks for all you do as priest and pastor. Where would we be without you? And I also want you to know that as we work together to make whole community catechesis a reality in the American Church, you who lead this work at the parish level are in our thoughts and prayers— indeed, how could it be otherwise?

Resources

Whole Community Catechesis Resources from Twenty-Third Publications

★ *The GDC in Plain English*, Bill Huebsch.

An outstanding summary of the *General Directory for Catechesis*.

★ *Whole Community Catechesis in Plain English*, Bill Huebsch.

The movement explained by the author who galvanized it.

★ *Handbook for Success in Whole Community Catechesis*, Bill Huebsch.

Practical guidelines for parish pastors and staff.

★ *Heritage of Faith: A Framework for Whole Community Catechesis*, Jo McClure Rotunno.

Background information plus Questions of the Week for all three liturgical cycles.

★ *Here Comes Everybody! Whole Community Catechesis in the Parish*, Leisa Anslinger.

A practical and inspiring testimony from a DRE who has experienced whole community catechesis.

★ *Increase Our Faith: Parish Prayer Services for Whole Community Catechesis, Year A*, David Haas.

Creative services for parish teams, parish councils, catechists, and all groups who meet in the parish; includes original music refrains.

★ *Let the Mystery Lead You: Bringing Catechesis and Liturgy Together*, Joe Paprocki and D. Todd Williamson.

An informative look at the essential links between teaching and worship.

Available in both Video and DVD formats

★ *7 Key Principals of Whole Community Catechesis*, presented by Bill Huebsch.

An excellent overview for parish pastors and staff.